GLASGOW'S LAST DAYS OF

by
W.A.C. Smith

Black Five 4-6-0 No. 45365 emerges from under Dobbie's Loan as it leaves Buchanan Street Station on 27 September 1963, the Glasgow autumn holiday weekend, with a 5.20 p.m. relief train for Aberdeen.

Text and photographs © W.A.C. Smith, 2003.
First published in the United Kingdom, 2003,
reprinted 2007
by Stenlake Publishing Ltd,
01290 551122
www.stenlake.co.uk

Printed by Adlard Print and Reprographics Ltd.

ISBN 9781840332698

The publishers regret that they cannot supply
copies of any pictures featured in this book.

Buchanan Street Station became a Mecca for enthusiasts in its final years before closure in November 1966, owing to the use of former London & North Eastern Railway class A4 Pacifics on the speeded-up Aberdeen trains – speeded-up, that is, to the three hour schedules which had applied in 1938/39. The station itself was of little architectural merit even after receiving platform canopies from the closed Ardrossan North Station in 1932, and a new wooden frontage. A4 No. 60034 'Lord Faringdon' is seen here on 31 May 1966, arriving five minutes early with the 1330 'Granite City' from Aberdeen, not the fastest of trains!

INTRODUCTION

The Garnkirk & Glasgow Railway heralded the arrival of the Railway Age in Scotland. Opened in 1831 to convey coal from the Monklands to Tennent's chemical works at Townhead, on the northern fringe of the city, and, unlike the pioneering horse-drawn waggonways which served mainly as adjuncts to the canal system, it set the pattern for future railway development with a passenger 'shed' at Glebe Street and being of double track worked by steam locomotives. In 1846 it was acquired by the newly formed Caledonian Railway and in 1847 was converted from the 4 feet 6 inch 'Scotch' gauge to the standard 4 feet 8½ inch gauge. Just two years later the Caledonian Railway built a line branching off the Garnkirk line at Provanmill and descending past St Rollox to a new terminus at Buchanan Street, more convenient to the city centre.

Meantime, however, the Glasgow, Paisley, Kilmarnock & Ayr Railway and the Glasgow, Paisley & Greenock Railway had been opened, in 1840 and 1841 respectively, from Bridge Street Station on the south side of the city and with a jointly owned line as far as Paisley. There was also a station at South Side, in the Gushetfaulds district, which was used by Caledonian trains from Lanarkshire, the Barrhead Railway, and, for a short time, by Anglo–Scottish services before these were diverted to Buchanan Street.

Early in 1842 Scotland's first intercity line was opened by the Edinburgh & Glasgow Railway which had Queen Street Station as its Glasgow terminus. The Cowlairs Incline, with 1¼ miles at a gradient of 1 in 41/43, was a formidable obstacle to trains leaving Queen Street and for many years rope haulage had to be used.

At this time Glasgow had no suburban services, but a rapid expansion of the city's boundaries from the mid-nineteenth century saw the opening, in 1866, of the Busby Railway (soon extended to East Kilbride) together with the Govan branch and followed in 1870 by the City of Glasgow Union Railway which, jointly owned by the North British and Glasgow & South Western railways, linked the railways north and south of the Clyde and gave access to a fine new terminal station at St Enoch opened by the Glasgow & South Western in 1876 (and enlarged in 1901). In 1877 a passenger service was inaugurated between Springburn and Govan, linking the main locomotive building centre in the city with the principal shipbuilding centre.

In 1879 the Caledonian Railway crossed the river for a new terminal, a second bridge was added and by 1906 the station had expanded to thirteen platforms and had become the Central Station we know today. A four-platform low level station had been added by the Glasgow Central Railway in 1896 as part of an enormously expensive Caledonian plan to serve the industrialised north bank of the Clyde by a line running parallel to that of the North British Railway, which had, in 1886, created a through east to west route, with a three-mile underground section and a low level station beneath their Queen Street terminal, by joining up various earlier railways by means of the Glasgow City & District Railway. This carried 15,000 passengers on its opening day and the Victorians, to quote from a contemporary press account, found a 'fearful joy in being whirled along under the streets of a great city.'

The City & District line was electrified by British Railways in 1960, by which time the rival Glasgow Central Railway was more or less moribund for, although the Caledonian Railway had obtained Parliamentary powers in 1898 for electrification, this was never carried out and there was a steady erosion of passengers to the Corporation Tramways after electrification of the latter took place between 1898 and 1901, this being followed by fifty years of expansion before replacement by buses commenced.

Under the London, Midland & Scottish Railway, a company created (together with the London & North Eastern Railway) by a government-instigated grouping of railway companies in 1923, new stations were opened in the Glasgow area at Kings Park, Croftfoot, Williamwood, Mosspark West and Hillington East and Hillington West. Plans for a passenger service over the Spiersbridge goods branch were aborted by the outbreak of the Second World War, during which travel by rail was actively discouraged, while the 1947 fuel crisis brought further cuts in services.

British Railways' monolithic management over the next twenty-five years, followed by incompetent privatisation and government indifference to the mounting problems, particularly of infrastructure, facing the railway industry at both local and national level, has resulted in the whole future of the network becoming under serious threat. On a day-to-day basis, the services provided by Scotrail and Strathclyde Passenger Transport are increasingly plagued by delays and cancellations while management procrastinates.

St Rollox Works was opened by the Caledonian Railway in 1856. A century later the works shunter was 0-4-0 saddle tank No. 56025 which, painted in mixed traffic black livery and fully lined out with the British Railways' emblem (rather than plain black), was kept in immaculate condition, as seen here on 25 April 1953. A small portion of the works remains in use today under private ownership, with the remainder of the site occupied by a supermarket.

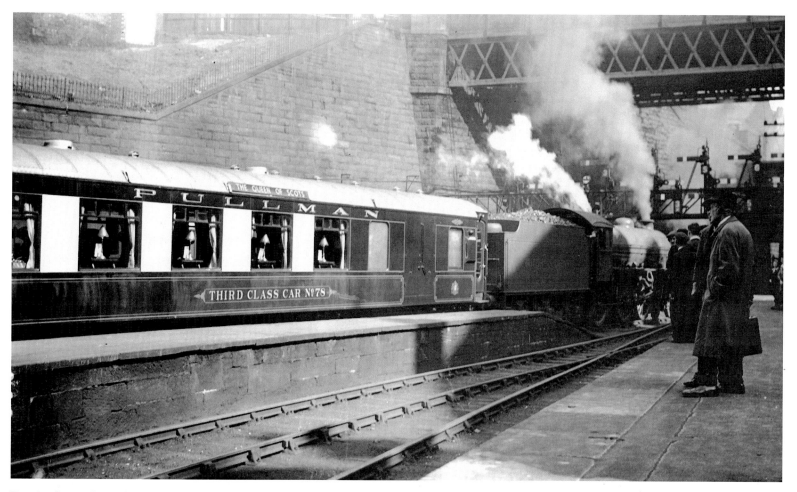

Despite Queen Street Station being a grimy, smoke-filled cavern, it was to the enthusiast a magical place of drifting smoke, roaring safety valves and raucous exhaust, compounded with admiration for staff struggling to maintain a semblance of the published timetables. It was also the scene of my first successful railway photograph! This was secured on 5 July 1948 when the prestigious 'Queen of Scots' Pullman, serving Edinburgh, Newcastle, Harrogate, Leeds and London King's Cross, resumed running after suspension during the Second World War. Motive Power on this occasion was class B1 4-6-0 No. 61328, newly-built by the North British Locomotive Company and resplendent in London & North Eastern Railway apple-green livery, soon to be replaced by BR black. Introduced in 1928, the train was withdrawn in 1964.

B1 4-6-0 No. 61140 awaits departure at platform two of Queen Street Station with the 1835 for Dunfermline Upper on 30 July 1965, and contrasts with one of the Swindon-built Intercity diesel multiple units which had taken over the Edinburgh and Glasgow service in 1957. The station's fine overall roof dates from 1878 and is 450 feet long, 250 feet wide and, at its highest point, almost 80 feet above the track level.

A pioneering concept by the Scottish Region was a 'television train' which entered service in 1956 for public excursions, school trips and private hire, and was made up of former London & North Eastern Railway coaching stock fitted with closed circuit television, studios and buffet facilities at Cowlairs Works. Films were shown on the train and there were live variety acts and interviews with passengers. With a banking locomotive assisting in rear, standard class 5 No. 73108 blasts up the Cowlairs Incline on 20 July 1957 with a 9.20 a.m. 'Evening Citizen' TV Show Train' from Queen Street to St Andrews. Unfortunately, with the inertia displayed at all times by the British Railways' Board, there was no place for an innovation such as this and the train ran for the last time in 1964. The Evening Citizen newspaper had already ceased publication because of TV competition!

The Cowlairs Incline, rising to 150 feet in 1¼ miles at a gradient of 1 in 41/43 and mainly in tunnel, was a formidable obstacle for trains leaving Queen Street and for many years rope haulage was resorted to (with special brake wagons for descending trains) until, in 1908, banking locomotives were successfully tried. Photographed on 2 September 1954, class D11 4-4-0 No. 62675 'Colonel Gardiner' tops the incline at Cowlairs Station with the 4.37 p.m. from Queen Street to Perth via Alloa and passes the former Winding House which contained the 80 horse-power high-pressure steam engine which powered the cable, guided by pulleys between the rails, used to haul trains (complete with their locomotives) out of Queen Street.

For half a century the North British Railway's 'A' class 0-6-2Ts were a familiar sight banking trains on the Cowlairs Incline, being fitted with a slip coupling arrangement comprising a wire from the front coupling leading along the boiler to a lever in the cab – at Cowlairs this was pulled to lift the link with the last coach of the train. Also to be seen in this photograph of class N14 No. 69120, at Eastfield shed on 12 September 1953, are the blinds which were fitted to the cabs of the banking engines in an attempt to keep out the choking smoke which filled the Cowlairs tunnel.

Eastfield depot was the largest on the North British system and was opened in 1904, prior to which there had been a small shed at Cowlairs, being situated alongside the Edinburgh and Glasgow main line. Rebuilt after being devastated by fire in 1919, steam was phased out in 1966 and final closure came in 1992. This photograph dates from 9 May 1953 and shows class V4 No. 61700 'Bantam Cock', one of a pair of lightweight 2-6-2s built at the London & North Eastern Railway's Doncaster Works in 1941 to a design of Sir Nigel Gresley. Following upon his untimely death, the new Chief Mechanical Engineer did not perpetuate the design, instead replacing it with the B1 4-6-0. Both No. 61700 and its twin (nicknamed 'Bantam Hen') were scrapped in 1957, having been very much 'odd job' locomotives during their relatively short working lives.

Although outwith the city boundary, Cadder Marshalling Yard dealt with much of the freight traffic for the north side of Glasgow and shunting locomotives, working twenty-four hours a day, were supplied by Eastfield Motive Power Depot while a one-coach staff train, known as the 'Cadder Bus', ran from Queen Street Station. Sited between Bishopbriggs and Lenzie and bisected by the Edinburgh and Glasgow main line, the yard had been opened by the North British Railway in 1901 to relieve chronic congestion at goods stations within the city, but British Railways' run down of freight traffic brought about its closure in the 1970s. On the evening of 27 July 1960 class J36 0-6-0 No. 65211 was photographed leaving with a transfer freight for Sighthill.

The former Glasgow & South Western Railway St Enoch terminus, modelled on that of the Midland Railway at St Pancras, had as its train of the day 'The Thames–Clyde Express' (the name dated from 1927) departing at 9.20 a.m. for London and calling en route at Kilmarnock, Dumfries, Carlisle, Leeds and Derby. From late in the London, Midland & Scottish era until dieselisation by British Railways, the latter event being proceeded briefly by the use of A3 Pacifics, the train was the preserve of rebuilt Royal Scot class 4-6-0s from Leeds Holbeck depot piloted in the up direction as far as Kilmarnock by a class 2P 4-4-0 from Hurlford depot, as seen in this photograph of 29 October 1952, which shows Nos. 40572 and 46103 'Royal Scots Fusilier' heading the train at platform one of St Enoch.

During the 1950s some of the local trains from St Enoch and Central stations were still being hauled by former Caledonian Railway 'tankies' (class 2P 0-4-4Ts) rather than the London, Midland & Scottish/British Railways' 'big pugs' (class 4MT 2-6-4Ts). Thus, on 28 October 1955, forty-three year old No. 55219 was leaving St Enoch with the 1.00 p.m. for Paisley (West).

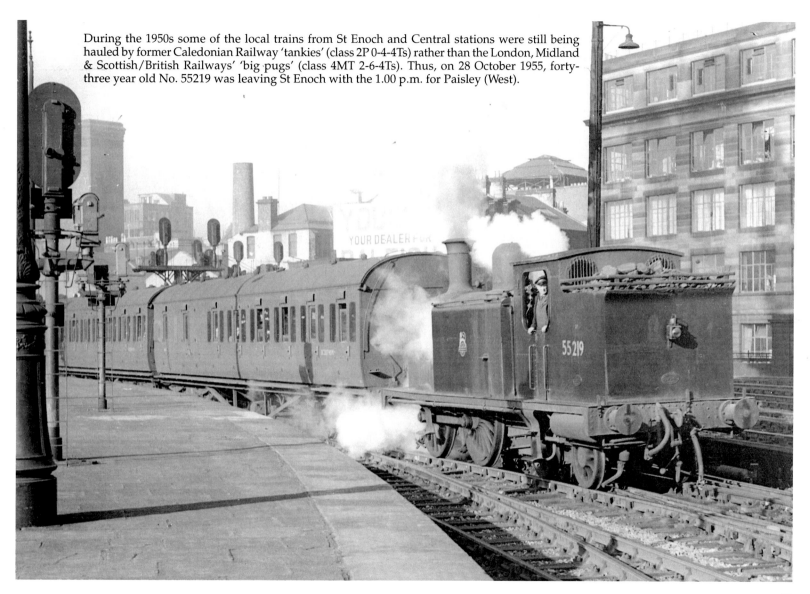

The 3.04 p.m. Saturdays-only train from St Enoch to Greenock Princes Pier was worked by a Corkerhill goods locomotive which returned with a cattle train from the Albert Harbour lairage at Greenock. On 18 July 1953 the 3.04 p.m. was photographed at platform eleven of St Enoch, headed by class 3F Caledonian Railway 0-6-0 No. 57560 which had been built at St Rollox Works in 1899.

Corkerhill Motive Power Depot (or 'shed' in everyday parlance) had an allocation of class 4P compound 4-4-0s, long since relegated from the main line expresses for which they had been built by the London, Midland & Scottish, and each summer these were joined by further members of the class, temporarily transferred from sheds ranging from Aberdeen to Dumfries, to work additional trains to the Ayrshire coast, in particular boat trains to the piers at Fairlie and Ardrossan. Thus, on Monday 26 September 1955, the Glasgow autumn holiday, No. 40909 was at platform twelve of St Enoch Station with the 9.50 a.m. for Fairlie Pier where it connected with the T.S. *Duchess of Hamilton* sailing to Campbeltown.

Latterly, St Enoch Station was a gloomy place, still with wartime blackout paint on the great arched roofs and platforms slippery with bird droppings. On 10 October 1959 standard class 5 No. 73104 was at platform three with the 10.45 a.m. departure for Girvan. Diesel multiple units took over the Ayrshire services three weeks later. St Enoch Station was closed in June 1966 and the site is now occupied by a shopping centre.

A countrywide strike by ASLEF members commenced at midnight on Saturday 28 May 1955 and ended seventeen days later, its principal achievement being an appreciable loss of freight traffic to road hauliers. The winners, apart from the road hauliers, were NUR members at former London, Midland & Scottish sheds where, if in sufficient numbers not to be intimidated by ASLEF pickets, were able to earn substantial overtime payments by working coal trains which were given priority. An emergency passenger timetable was published in the press on a daily basis, and on 30 May class 4MT 2-6-4T No. 42202 was photographed leaving platform two at a deserted St Enoch Station at 5.40 p.m. with a ten-coach train for Ayr. The only other services from St Enoch that evening were at 5.13 and 5.55 to Greenock Princes Pier, 5.38 to Dumfries, 7.50 to Ayr and 9.05 to Dumfries.

The transition from steam to diesel traction is well illustrated in this symbolic shot, taken at Central Station on the late evening of 14 June 1957 and showing the 1897-built Caledonian class 2F 0-6-0 No. 57463 shunting luggage vans while London, Midland & Scottish-built diesels Nos. 10000 and 10001 are about to depart with the 9.25 p.m. sleeping car train for London Euston. These were Britain's first main line diesel locomotives, with No. 10000 entering service in 1947 only weeks before nationalisation of the 'Big Four' railway companies. Both were withdrawn in the mid-1960s, having outlived sixty-four year old No. 57463 by less than five years!

Opposite: In 1937 the London, Midland & Scottish Railway introduced the streamlined 'Coronation Scot' train between London Euston and Glasgow Central with a 1.30 p.m. departure time and a six and a half hour schedule. This ceased to run because of the war and a long overdue (no pun intended) replacement was not put on by British Railways until the summer of 1957. Named 'The Caledonian', it left Glasgow at 8.30 a.m., was restricted to eight coaches and, calling only at Carlisle, took six hours and forty minutes for the 401 miles. It proved popular and the following year was joined by a second train, leaving at 4.00 p.m., the inaugural working of which took place on 9 June 1958 and is shown here leaving from platform three at Central Station hauled by Coronation Pacific No. 46232, 'Duchess of Montrose'. Platform two is occupied by the 4.05 p.m. service to Liverpool and Manchester headed by Britannia Pacific No. 70051, 'Firth of Forth'. Unfortunately, patronage of the new train was poor and it was soon taken off, the morning train following suite in the early 1960s owing to electrification work taking place south of Crewe.

As previously mentioned, former Caledonian Railway locomotives continued to be seen on suburban services around Glasgow well into the British Railways era, and on 24 September 1958 class 3F 0-6-0 No. 57581 was photographed leaving Central Station with the 5.51 p.m. train for Kirkhill. Built in 1900 by Neilson, Reid and Co., No. 57581 was withdrawn for scrapping in September 1963.

New British Railways' standard class 4MT 2-6-4Ts began to appear in Scotland early in 1952 and were soon a familiar sight in the Glasgow area. In this photograph No. 80115 is seen leaving Central Station on 25 May 1962 with the 5.36 p.m. to Kirkhill, but line closures, together with increasing dieselisation and electrification, gave these locomotives very short working lives and this particular locomotive, built in 1954, was scrapped in 1964.

The crew of class 2F 0-6-0 No. 57446 have built up a good head of steam for the climb to East Kilbride and are briefly taking things easy as the veteran Caledonian Jumbo charges over Pollokshields East Junction with the 6.21 p.m. train from Central Station on 1 August 1957. East Kilbride trains were diverted to St Enoch Station in 1959, but reverted to Central Station in 1966, and the junction (where the Cathcart Outer Circle parts company with the Glasgow, Barrhead & Kilmarnock line) is now known as Muirhouse North Junction.

The Cathcart Circle, completed in 1894 by the Caledonian Railway (in the guise of the Cathcart District Railway), was for many years an institution in the life of the city's south side and had a novel written about it (*Snooker Tam of the Cathcart Railway* by R.W. Campbell, published in 1919), dealt with thousands of football fans at Mount Florida Station on occasions of big matches at Hampden Park, and even possessed its own amateur team in the 1930s. Motive power was equally varied and on 5 July 1957 class 4F 0-6-0 No. 44001, essentially a freight locomotive, was photographed at Langside & Newlands Station with the 8.30 p.m. outer circle train from Central Station. This train was rostered for a Corkerhill, rather than a Polmadie, locomotive and crew.

The highlights of Friday evenings in the 1950s for railway enthusiasts were the 'Starlight Specials' (see front cover caption). On 15 July 1955 class 2P 4-4-0 No. 40573 and Jubilee 4-6-0 No. 45573 'Newfoundland' accelerate through Strathbungo with a 7.45 p.m. 'Starlight' from St Enoch. The pilot locomotive was detached at New Cumnock. Strathbungo Station, opened in 1877, was closed in 1962 upon implementation of the Glasgow South electrification scheme.

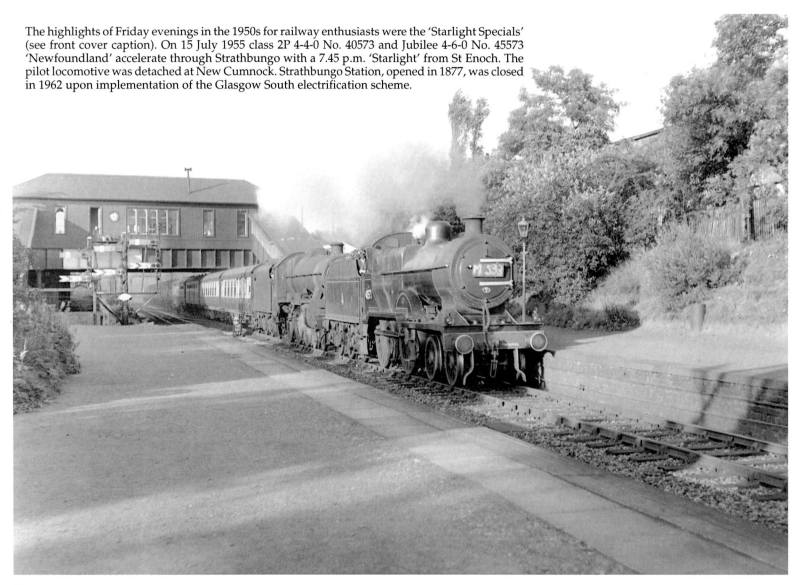

Pacifics were the elite of steam locomotives and, although occasionally seen at Corkerhill and Eastfield sheds, with several allocated to Balornock in the final years of steam, the elite of the elite were the magnificent Stanier Pacifics of the London, Midland & Scottish, construction of which had commenced at Crewe works in 1937. By the mid-1950s Glasgow's Polmadie depot had nine of these magnificent machines among its allocation of 170 or more steam locomotives. Photographed on 8 May 1954, No. 46232 'Duchess of Montrose' was coming off shed to work one of the heavy overnight sleeper trains. She went to the scrap heap, many thought prematurely, at the end of 1962.

By 1955 the number of Pacifics at Polmadie had been increased to nineteen by the arrival of five each of British Railways' new Britannias (class 7MT) and Clans (class 6MT), all built at Crewe Works. Britannia No. 70054, 'Dornoch Firth', was photographed on 25 June 1955 and was the last of the class to be built. It was transferred away from Polmadie in 1958 and went for scrap in 1966.

No. 72000, 'Clan Buchanan', named by the city's Lord Provost at Central Station in January 1952, was photographed at Polmadie on 9 April 1955. The MT (mixed traffic) power classification carried by these locomotives proved symbolic as they had a mixed reputation throughout their working lives of around fifteen years. Some footplate crews found them to be indifferent performers while others thought them free steaming, and fitters appreciated their ease of maintenance.

Goods stations were the life blood of the railways and were strategically placed in and around the city centre with those of Caledonian and Glasgow & South Western origin being, in British Railways' days, almost invariably shunted by former Caledonian Railway 782 class 0-6-0Ts, 138 of which were built between 1898 and 1922. These humble workhorses tended to be ignored by enthusiasts, but on 27 April 1960 I photographed No. 56308 at South Side in the Gorbals district of the city. Soon, however, such pugs had been replaced by diesel shunters, followed by elimination of the goods stations themselves.

Over the years I have (by chance) occupied several houses overlooking railway lines. Of these desirable residences – desirable, that is, for anyone interested in railways – one, occupied for several years during the steam era, was in the Pollokshields district and, situated alongside the Paisley Canal line, faced Bellahouston No. 1 signal box which controlled both the exit from Bellahouston carriage sidings and a connection from the Clydesdale line. For good measure a backdrop was also provided by the Paisley Joint line. Photography was possible from my kitchen window and this picture, taken on 12 July 1956, shows former Caledonian Railway 4-4-0 No. 54506, from Greenock Princes Pier shed, leaving the carriage sidings with empty coaches for St Enoch Station. The site is now occupied by Shields Electric Traction Depot.

In 1893 the Glasgow & South Western opened a connecting line from the City Union to the North British Railway Bridgeton Cross branch with a frequent, but short-lived, service of 'bus trains' from Bellahouston & Dumbreck Station on the Paisley Canal line. A third platform was installed for these trains and the remains of this can be seen in this photograph taken on 16 September 1954, which also shows class 4MT 2-6-4T No. 42124 leaving with the 5.36 p.m. from St Enoch to Greenock Princes Pier. The station was closed just two days later, but when the Paisley Canal line was reopened in 1990, after a seven year closure, a new station (named Dumbreck) was provided on a slightly different site.

Rarely seen, and little known even to train-spotters of the period, were several former Highland Railway 0-6-0s dating from the early 1900s (and nicknamed 'Barneys', for reasons unknown). These arrived at Corkerhill shed in 1946/47 where they were regarded as worn out and were restricted to occasional appearances on local freight trips. Although all had gone for scrap by 1952, I had secured a photograph of No. 57695 at Corkerhill shed on 2 September 1950. None of these engines survived long enough to receive the British Railways lion and wheel emblem on the tender.

Thanks to having an unusually enterprising General Manager at the time – James Ness – the Scottish Region restored four historic locomotives to working order in 1958/59. These – Caledonian Railway 4-2-2 No. 123, North British Railway 4-4-0 No. 256, 'Glen Douglas', Great North of Scotland Railway 4-4-0 No. 49, 'Gordon Highlander', and Highland Railway 4-6-0 No. 103 – are pictured at Dawsholm locomotive shed on the occasion of a press preview on 17 August 1959. The diesel multiple unit had brought the special party from Buchanan Street Station. Dawsholm shed, at Maryhill, dated from the opening of the Glasgow Central Low Level system in the mid-1890s, and closed with it in 1964.

The preserved locomotives were used for a series of excursions in connection with the Scottish Industries Exhibition held in the Kelvin Hall during September 1959 and Nos. 49 and 103 are seen taking to the Clydesdale line at Shields Junction with one such train from Ayr bound for Kelvin Hall Station (formerly Partick Central) on the Glasgow Central Low Level line. No. 49 was built in 1920 by the North British Locomotive Company for the Great North of Scotland Railway and No. 103, the pioneer locomotive of the 4-6-0 wheel arrangement in this country, had come from Sharp, Stewart & Co. in 1894 for the Highland Railway. Both are now in the Glasgow Museum of Transport.

The City Union line gave the North British Railway access to Terminus Quay, Princes Dock, Govan, Shieldhall, Paisley Greenlaw and Elderslie Yard for goods traffic, and such workings from Parkhead shed continued well into British Railways' days. On 7 May 1953 class J39 0-6-0 No. 64847, fresh from overhaul at Cowlairs Works, was photographed joining the four-track Paisley Joint line at Ibrox with a train from the Govan branch which had lost its passenger service as early as 1902.

The City Union was also frequently used by special passenger trains and, when Rangers F.C. were playing at home, a pair of well-patronised football specials were run from Springburn to Ibrox by means of this line. On 5 September 1959 class K2 2-6-0 No. 61772, 'Loch Lochy', a type more often seen on the West Highland line, was photographed returning from Ibrox to Springburn with the second train (punctually at 5.06 p.m.), the first having left behind B1 4-6-0 No. 61342. There were also several specials that evening for Glasgow Central worked by 2-6-4Ts. Unfortunately, such traffic was lost to rail by the closure of Ibrox Station in 1967.

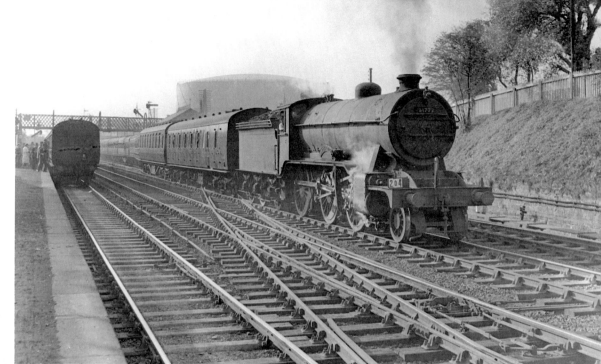

At Ibrox on 29 May 1954 class 5MT 2-6-0 No. 42742 restarts the 2.36 p.m. from St Enoch to Ardrossan Town. These rather odd looking locomotives, introduced by the London, Midland & Scottish Railway in 1926 and soon nicknamed 'Crabs', were mainly used on freight work with several running in Ayrshire until late in 1966.

Partick, on the north side of the Clyde, is situated opposite Govan and when shipbuilders J. & G. Thomson moved from Govan to a much larger yard at Clydebank (and became better known as John Brown's), a station was established at Partick in 1882 by the Glasgow, Yoker & Clydebank Railway to convey the workers to the new shipyard. The line later formed part of the Glasgow City & District system, being extended to Dalmuir and forming a useful alternative to the 1858 Helensburgh Railway. Partick was renamed Partick Hill in 1952 to avoid confusion with stations on the Central Low Level line but, when resited in 1979, it once again became Partick. On 22 March 1960 class V1 2-6-2T No. 67616 was photographed at Partick Hill with the 2.18 p.m. from Jordanhill to Bridgeton Central.

A short branch from Partick Junction to Hyndland (a projected extension to Botanic Gardens was not proceeded with) was built as part of the Glasgow City & District Railway, which was opened in 1886 through Queen Street Low Level Station and had trains to Edinburgh until closure of the Bathgate route in 1956. With electrification from Airdrie, Springburn and Bridgeton to Milngavie, Helensburgh and Balloch, a new station was provided on the through line and the original station at Hyndland became a depot for the Blue Trains. On 15 July 1960 V1 2-6-2T No. 67633 was photographed heading the 5.22 p.m. for Airdrie while new electric trains in their attractive Caledonian blue livery awaited entry into service. This depot has now been replaced by one at Yoker.

The class K3 2-6-0s, 193 in total, were built in the 1920s and 30s, firstly by the Great Northern Railway and then by the London & North Eastern Railway, for express freight work. Photographed on 15 April 1960, No. 61987 is seen awaiting departure from Partick Hill goods station with one such train.

However, scrapping of the class had already commenced as this melancholy view of No. 61909, in Cowlairs Works yard on 29 April 1960, testifies.

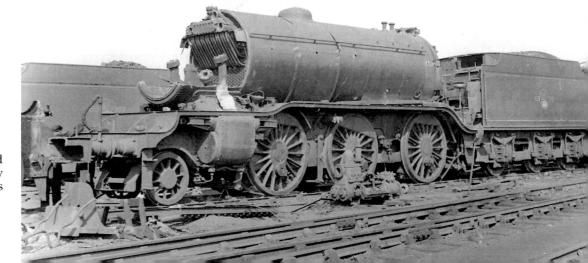

Scotstounhill Station, on the Glasgow, Yoker & Clydebank Railway, was opened in 1883. Seventy-five years later, on 20 August 1958, V3 No. 67612 called with the 3.37 p.m. train from Bridgeton Central to Clydebank East. For thirty years these London & North Eastern Railway class V1 and V3 2-6-2Ts (they were identical, but for the V3s having a higher boiler pressure) were a familiar sight, and sound, on the Queen Street Low Level line.

On 24 July 1958 standard class 4MT 2-6-0 No. 76074 approaches Knightswood South Junction with a workers train from Singer to Bridgeton Central. It is using a City & District spur from Knightswood North Junction which linked the Glasgow, Dumbarton & Helensburgh Railway with the Stobcross branch of the North British Railway. The Knightswood goods branch is on the left.

At its east end the City & District Railway connected at Bellgrove with both the City Union line and the Coatbridge branch of the Edinburgh & Glasgow Railway to which Carntyne Station was added in 1888. This photograph was taken on 7 May 1956 and shows V3 2-6-2T No. 67611 arriving at Carntyne with the 11.35 a.m. from Hyndland to Easterhouse.

A North British Railway monopoly of traffic to and from the docks and industrial establishments along the north bank of the Clyde was rudely broken in 1896 when the Caledonian Railway penetrated the area with two nominally independent companies. These were the Glasgow Central Railway, with a lengthy underground section beneath Argyle Street, and the Lanarkshire & Dunbartonshire Railway which joined at Maryhill with an existing goods line round the north side of the city. Ex-London, Midland & Scottish class 3MT 2-6-2T No. 40187 is seen in this photograph, taken on 21 August 1957 at Partick West Station where there was a triangular junction with the Maryhill line, heading the 5.16 p.m. from Dalmuir Riverside to Carmyle. The cattle waggons on the right are in the sidings at Merklands lairage which were opened in 1907 for the landing of Irish cattle. Today, the site of the station is occupied by the Clydeside Expressway.

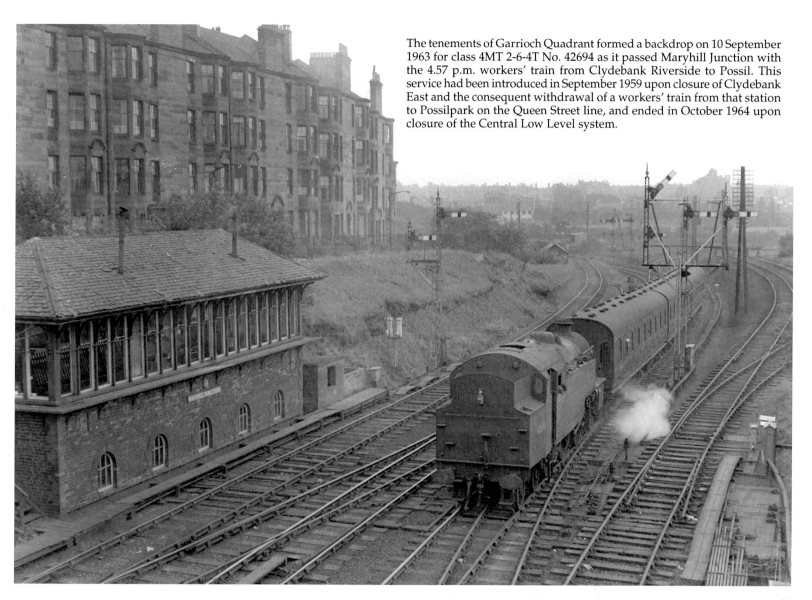

The tenements of Garrioch Quadrant formed a backdrop on 10 September 1963 for class 4MT 2-6-4T No. 42694 as it passed Maryhill Junction with the 4.57 p.m. workers' train from Clydebank Riverside to Possil. This service had been introduced in September 1959 upon closure of Clydebank East and the consequent withdrawal of a workers' train from that station to Possilpark on the Queen Street line, and ended in October 1964 upon closure of the Central Low Level system.

The Clyde saw its first steamboat in 1812 and soon thirty or more paddle steamers were plying from the Broomielaw to the Clyde coast, with others sailing to Liverpool and Ireland. However, the opening of railway piers began a decline in 'all the way' sailings and by the 1930s only Williamson–Buchanan Steamers and David MacBrayne Ltd, the latter with its long-established 'Royal Route' sailing at 7.11 a.m., were providing such services which, in 1929, had been transferred from the Broomielaw to Bridge Wharf on the south side of the river. Post-war sailings were made by the Caledonian Steam Packet Company, but ended in 1969. Today, the preserved P.S. *Waverley* provides limited down-river sailings from Anderston Quay. On 2 June 1956 the MacBrayne turbine steamer *King George V* made a charter sailing from Bridge Wharf and I photographed her return that evening.

The North British Locomotive Co. Ltd was formed in 1903 by amalgamation of Neilson, Reid & Co., Sharp Stewart & Co. and Dubs & Co. and, until liquidation in 1962, built 28,000 locomotives, 18,000 of them for export. With many bound for overseas railways, their passage from Springburn through the city streets to the docks, hauled by a pair of steam traction engines, was a familiar sight. However, by September 1951, when this photograph was taken at Stobcross Quay, a Scammell diesel tractor was being used. The locomotive is 4-6-4 No. R742, built for the 5 feet 3 inch gauge Victoria Government Railways of Australia, one of seventy of this type built between 1950 and 1952.

During the 1950s forty-two oil-fired 3 feet 6 inch gauge 4-8-2s were built for Sudan Railways and, on 17 June 1955, Nos. 528 to 533 were to be seen at Stobcross Quay awaiting shipment. This was the North British Locomotive Co.'s last big steam order.

For many years Provan Gas Works on the north side of the city had a 2 feet 6 inch gauge rail system, used for servicing the retorts. One of the diminutive locomotives, No. 1, built by Andrew Barclay & Co. Ltd of Kilmarnock in 1946, was photographed on 5 June 1954. The system closed down five years later.

Standard gauge (4 feet 8½ inches) railway wagons could be worked on their flanges over the 4 feet 7¾ inch gauge Glasgow Corporation Tramways. Such was the practice in Renfrew Road, where an 0-4-0 saddle tank locomotive belonging to Alexander Stephen & Sons Ltd, en route from the Linthouse Shipyard to Shieldhall goods station, was photographed passing tram No. 1391 on service 27 (Shieldhall to Springburn). The date was 26 February 1958. The pug had been built by Andrew Barclay & Co. Ltd in 1924 while the Cunarder tram came from the Corporation's Coplawhill tram works in 1951. The last tram ran in Glasgow in 1962, and the Linthouse Shipyard closed in 1968.

British Railways came into existence on 1 January 1948 with its Scottish Region having an allocation of 2,300 steam locomotives. Ongoing dieselisation and electrification, together with line closures, had reduced this figure to sixty-two by 1 January 1967 and on and from Monday 1 May of that year steam working within the Region was eliminated. The ten remaining steam passenger trains at Glasgow's Central Station, all Saturdays excepted and principally on the Gourock line, were replaced by diesel multiple units after 28 April; the station pilots at Central Station and the Beattock bankers were dieselised the following day. Although occasional visits by London Midland Region steam locomotives continued until closure of Kingmoor Motive Power Depot at Carlisle on 31 December 1967, the last Scottish Region passenger train to be steam hauled was the 1703 from Gourock on Friday 28 April, an historic event but devoid of ceremony. After this service's arrival at platform twelve of Central Station, punctually at 1807, I photographed class 4MT 2-6-4T No. 42274 propelling out with the empty stock bound for Smithy Lye sidings at Shields Road.

The evening of the following day (Saturday 29 April 1967) brought 136 years of main line steam traction in Scotland to an end when standard 2-6-4T No. 80116, acting as pilot at Larkfield carriage sidings at Gushetfaulds, returned to Polmadie depot for the last time. It was photographed at Larkfield shortly before finishing work that evening.

The run down of British Railways steam brought an upsurge of interest in railway preservation. Among locomotives saved from the scrap heap was class 3F 0-6-0 No. 57566, built at St Rollox Works in 1899 as Caledonian Railway No. 828 and acquired in 1963 by the Scottish Locomotive Preservation Fund. After a period in store it was repainted in its original blue livery at Cowlairs Works in 1966, being moved to Govan goods station and thence, by low loader on 22 August, to the Glasgow Museum of Transport which at that time was situated in Pollokshields. Since restored to working order, No. 828 is now on the Strathspey Railway at Aviemore.